Glow 15 Unofficial

Recipe Book:

30 More Tantalizing,

Healthy, Energizing

Recipes

By

Karah Westlake

Grab Your Free Bonus Now

Thank you for purchasing this book! You can get your free
gift here:

Free Special Recipes Collection

Download It Immediately Here:

http://cookbooks247.com/bonus

Glow 15 Recipe Book

Contents

Salt and Vinegar Bok Choy

Herbed Green Smoothie

Miso-Glazed Brussels Sprouts

Citrus Carrots

Berries and Dandelion Smoothie

Sautéed Cauliflower

Roasted Tomatoes

GLOW 15 AUTOPHASAUCES RECIPES

Special Avocado Dip

Black Beans Dip

Spinach Dip

Parsley and Basil Dip

Olives and Cherry Tomatoes Dip

Maple-Scented Tahini Dip

Miso Almond Dip

Greens Pesto

Avocado Cheese Dip

Yogurt Dip

GLOW 15 Recipe Book Grocery List:

Shrimp Lettuce Wraps

Crunchy Chicken

Turkey Salad

Delicious Whole Chicken

Stir Fried Broccoli and Salmon

Chicken Stew

Beef with Mixed Herb Butter

Pork and Beans Chili

Broiled Tilapia

Turkey Meatballs

Beef Sirloin Steak

Broccoli Avocado Salad

Spinach and Fruits Salad

Asparagus Soup

Grilled Veggies

Salt and Vinegar Bok Choy

Herbed Green Smoothie

Miso-Glazed Brussels Sprouts

Citrus Carrots

Berries and Dandelion Smoothie

Sautéed Cauliflower

Roasted Tomatoes

Special Avocado Dip

Black Beans Dip

Spinach Dip

Parsley and Basil Dip

Olives and Cherry Tomatoes Dip

Maple-Scented Tahini Dip

Miso Almond Dip

Greens Pesto

Avocado Cheese Dip

Yogurt Dip

Grab Your Free Bonus Now

FINAL SURPRISE BONUS

GLOW 15 HIGH-DAY

RECIPES

Shrimp Lettuce Wraps

Servings: 10

Preparation Time: 20 minutes

Cooking Time: 10 minutes

Total Time: 30 minutes

Ingredients:

- 1 pound shrimps

- 2 tablespoons extra-virgin olive oil

- 2 garlic cloves, minced

- 1 green bell pepper, seeded and chopped

- ½ cup summer squash, chopped

- ½ teaspoon curry powder

- 1 onion, chopped

- 1 cup carrot, peeled and chopped

- ½ cup zucchini, chopped

- 2 tablespoons low-sodium soy sauce

- Freshly ground black pepper, to taste

- 10 large lettuce leaves

Directions:

1. Heat oil in a large skillet over medium heat and add shrimps.

2. Cook for about 5 minutes, breaking the lumps.

3. Stir in the vegetables and cook for about 4 minutes.

4. Add soy sauce, curry powder and black pepper and cook for about 5 minutes.

5. Remove from heat and keep aside to cool slightly.

6. Place the lettuce leaves onto serving plates and divide the shrimp mixture evenly over the leaves.

7. Serve these yummy lettuce wraps immediately.

Nutritional Value:

Calories 97

Total Fat 3.7 g

Saturated Fat 0.6 g

Cholesterol 96 mg

Sodium 297 mg

Total Carbs 5.1 g

Fiber 0.9 g

Sugar 2.3 g

Protein 11.1 g

Potassium 204 mg

Crunchy Chicken

Servings: 4

Prep Time: 10 minutes

Cooking Time: 10 minutes

Total Time: 20 minutes

Ingredients:

- 8 skinless, boneless chicken tenderloins

- 2 tablespoons tea seed oil

- 2 tablespoons low-fat yogurt

- 1 teaspoon turmeric powder

- Salt and freshly ground black pepper, to taste

Directions:

1. Mix yogurt with salt, black pepper and turmeric powder.

2. Season the chicken tenderloins in the marinade.

3. Preheat the air fryer to 355°F and coat the baking dish with tea seed oil.

4. Put the chicken tenderloins in the air fryer and cook for about 10 minutes.

5. Dish out and serve with mint dip.

Nutritional Information per Serving:

Calories 342

Total Fat 14.9 g

Saturated Fat 4.4 g

Cholesterol 130 mg

Sodium 80 mg

Total Carbs 0.4 g

Sugar 0 g

Fiber 0.1 g

Potassium 14 mg

Protein 50 g

Turkey Salad

Servings: 3

Preparation Time: 10 minutes

Cooking Time: 0 minutes

Total Time: 10 minutes

Ingredients:

- 5 ounce turkey meat, cooked

- 2 tablespoons tahini

- ¼ cup celery, chopped

- 2 tablespoons avocado mayonnaise

- ½ lemon, juiced

- ½ teaspoon ground turmeric

- 1 cup broccoli sprouts

- Freshly ground pepper, to taste

Directions:

1. Mix together all the ingredients in a large bowl except broccoli sprouts.

2. Top with broccoli sprouts and transfer into a serving bowl.

3. Serve immediately with your favorite smoothie.

Nutritional Value:

Calories 168

Total Fat 9.1 g

Saturated Fat 1.8 g

Cholesterol 36 mg

Sodium 62 mg

Total Carbs 6 g

Fiber 2.6 g

Sugar 1 g

Protein 16.7 g

Potassium 352 mg

Delicious Whole Chicken

Servings: 4

Preparation Time: 10 minutes

Cooking Time: 25 minutes

Total Time: 35 minutes

Ingredients:

- ½ tablespoon fresh rosemary, minced

- 1 teaspoon ground cumin

- 1 teaspoon cayenne pepper

- 1 teaspoon red pepper flakes, crushed

- Salt and freshly ground black pepper, to taste

- 1 pound organic whole chicken, neck and giblet removed

- 1 tablespoon tea seed oil

Directions:

1. Mix together rosemary, ground cumin, cayenne pepper, red pepper flakes, salt and black pepper in a bowl.

2. Rub the chicken generously with the spice mixture.

3. Place the tea seed oil in the Instant Pot and select "Sauté".

4. Add the chicken and sauté for about 3 minutes or until browned from all sides.

5. Select the "Cancel" and lock the lid.

6. Select "Poultry" and just use the default time of 12 minutes.

7. Select the "Cancel" and carefully do a Quick pressure release.

8. Remove the lid and flip the side of chicken.

9. Secure the lid and cook under "Manual" and "High Pressure" for about 10 minutes.

10. Select the "Cancel" and carefully release the pressure quickly.

11. Remove the lid and place chicken onto a cutting board for about 10 minutes before carving.

12. Cut chicken into desires sized pieces with a sharp knife and serve immediately.

Nutritional Value:

Calories 207

Total Fat 7 g

Saturated Fat 1.4 g

Cholesterol 87 mg

Sodium 73 mg

Total Carbs 1 g

Fiber 0.5 g

Sugar 0.1 g

Protein 33.1 g

Potassium 244 mg

Stir Fried Broccoli and Salmon

Servings: 5

Preparation Time: 15 minutes

Cooking Time: 10 minutes

Total Time: 25 minutes

Ingredients:

- 1 pound salmon, chunked

- 2 garlic cloves, minced

- 1 tablespoon gluten free coconut aminos

- 1 tablespoon dark sesame oil

- 5 cups broccoli, chopped

- ¾ teaspoon red pepper flakes

- 3 scallions, thinly sliced

- 1-inch piece fresh ginger, minced

- 3 tablespoons tea seed oil

- Salt and freshly ground black pepper, to taste

- 2 tablespoons sesame seeds

Directions:

1. Mix together salmon chunks, half the garlic, scallions, sesame oil and coconut aminos in a bowl and toss well.

2. Refrigerate the mixture for about 1 hour.

3. Heat 1 tablespoon tea seed oil in a large skillet over high heat and add broccoli.

4. Cook for 30 seconds and add garlic, ginger, 2 tablespoons water, salt and black pepper.

5. Cook for about 3 minutes and dish out in a plate.

6. Heat the remaining tea seed oil in the same skillet over medium heat and add red pepper flakes and salmon chunks.

7. Cook for about 3 minutes and add cooked broccoli and 2 tablespoons water.

8. Cook for about 2 more minutes and dish out in 4 plates.

9. Sprinkle with sesame seeds and serve with topping of your choice.

Nutritional Value:

Calories 276

Total Fat 18.3 g

Saturated Fat 2.4 g

Cholesterol 40 mg

Sodium 80 mg

Total Carbs 8.7 g

Fiber 3.1 g

Sugar 1.8 g

Protein 21.1 g

Potassium 688 mg

Chicken Stew

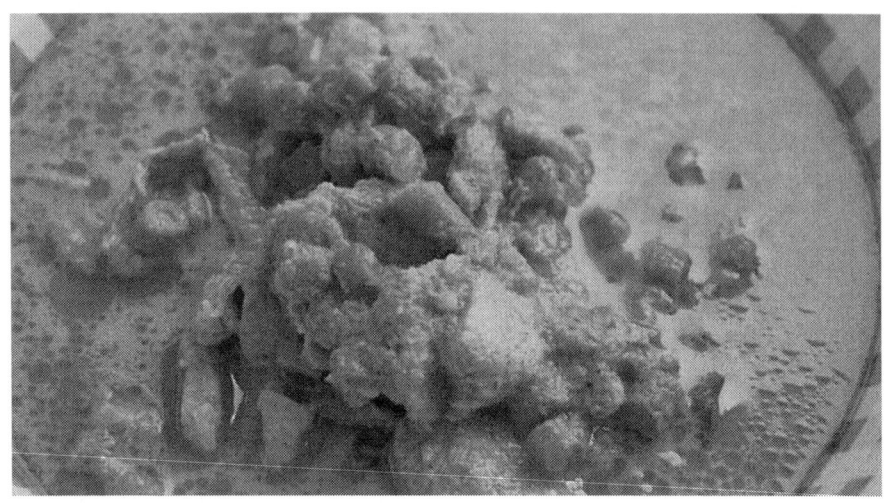

Servings: 6

Preparation Time: 12 minutes

Cooking time: 16 minutes

Total Time: 28 minutes

Ingredients:

- 1 tablespoon tea seed oil

- 1 pound fresh mushrooms, quartered

- 1 small yellow onion, chopped

- 3 garlic cloves, minced

- 6 (5-ounce) grass-fed skinless, boneless chicken thighs

- 1 cup green olives, pitted

- 1 tablespoon sugar-free tomato paste

- 2 cups fresh cherry tomatoes, halved

- 1 cup homemade chicken broth

- ½ cup water

- Salt and black pepper, to taste

- ¼ cup parsley, chopped

Directions:

1. Place the oil in the Instant Pot and press "Sauté" button.

2. Add the onions, garlic and mushrooms and cook for about 5 minutes.

3. Stir in tomato paste and cook for about 1 minute.

4. Add the chicken, olives, tomatoes, water and broth.

5. Set the Instant Pot to "Manual" and "High Pressure" for about 10 minutes.

6. Release the pressure naturally and unlock the lid.

7. Season generously with salt, black pepper and parsley.

8. Dish out in a large serving bowl and serve hot to your guests.

Nutritional Value:

Calories 242

Total Fat 10.5 g

Saturated Fat 2.2 g

Cholesterol 101 mg

Sodium 271 mg

Total Carbs 7.4 g

Fiber 2 g

Sugar 3.9 g

Protein 31.9 g

Potassium 482 mg

Beef with Mixed Herb Butter

Servings: 4

Preparation Time: 5 minutes

Cooking Time: 20 minutes

Total Time: 25 minutes

Ingredients:

- 4 (6-ounce) beef steaks

- 1 lemon, halved

- 2 teaspoons fresh dill, chopped

- 2½ tablespoons unsalted butter

- 2 teaspoons fresh thyme

- 2 garlic cloves, minced

- Salt and freshly ground black pepper, to taste

Directions:

1. Preheat the broiler to high and line a baking sheet with parchment paper.

2. Place the beef steaks on the parchment and top with butter.

3. Squeeze the lemon juice over the beef steaks and season with thyme, dill, garlic, salt and black pepper.

4. Broil for 20 minutes and dish out in the serving plates.

5. Top the steaks with unsalted butter and dish out in a bowl.

6. Serve immediately to your guests.

Nutritional Value:

Calories 389

Total Fat 17.9 g

Saturated Fat 8.6 g

Cholesterol 171 mg

Sodium 165 mg

Total Carbs 2.5 g

Fiber 0.7 g

Sugar 0.4 g

Protein 52.1 g

Potassium 734 mg

Pork and Beans Chili

Servings: 8

Preparation Time: 20 minutes

Cooking Time: 50 minutes

Total Time: 1 hour 10 minutes

Ingredients:

- 2 pounds grass-fed pork, ground

- 2 garlic cloves, minced

- 3 teaspoons red chili powder

- 1 (15-ounce) can black beans, rinsed and drained

- 3 cups fresh baby spinach

- 6-ounce tomato paste

- 1 tablespoon tea seed oil

- ¼ cup onion, chopped

- 1 teaspoon fresh ginger, minced

- 1 teaspoon dried thyme

- 1 teaspoon ground cumin

- 3 tomatoes, chopped

- 1 cup water

Directions:

1. Heat oil in a large pan over medium heat and add pork.

2. Cook for about 5 minutes and add onion, garlic, ginger, thyme and spices.

3. Sauté for about 3 minutes and stir in the remaining ingredients.

4. Cook for about 5 minutes until boiling and reduce the flame.

5. Simmer, covered for about 40 minutes, occasionally stirring.

6. Dish out in a serving bowl and serve hot.

Nutritional Value:

Calories 290

Total Fat 14.2 g

Saturated Fat 4.7 g

Cholesterol 53 mg

Sodium 85 mg

Total Carbs 20.3 g

Fiber 6.8 g

Sugar 4.1 g

Protein 21.2 g

Potassium 817 mg

Broiled Tilapia

Servings: 8

Preparation Time: 20 minutes

Cooking Time: 5 minutes

Total Time: 25 minutes

Ingredients:

- ½ cup Pecorino Romano cheese, grated

- 2 tablespoons avocado mayonnaise

- 2 tablespoons tea seed oil

- 2 tablespoons fresh lemon juice

- 2 pounds tilapia fillets

- ¼ teaspoon dried thyme

- Salt and freshly ground black pepper, to taste

Directions:

1. Preheat the oven to broiler and grease a broiler pan.

2. Mix together all the ingredients in a large bowl except tilapia fillets.

3. Place the fillets onto prepared broiler pan in a single layer.

4. Broil the fillets for about 3 minutes and remove from oven.

5. Top the fillets with cheese mixture evenly and broil for about 2 minutes more.

6. Dish onto a serving platter and immediately serve.

Nutritional Value:

Calories 163

Total Fat 7.1 g

Saturated Fat 2.5 g

Cholesterol 64 mg

Sodium 148 mg

Total Carbs 0.6 g

Fiber 0.2 g

Sugar 0.2 g

Protein 24 g

Potassium 24 mg

Turkey Meatballs

Servings: 8

Preparation Time: 15 minutes

Cooking Time: 10 minutes

Total Time: 25 minutes

Ingredients:

- 1 cup cooked black beans, mashed roughly

- ½ cup fresh parsley, chopped

- Tea seed oil, as required

- 1 pound extra-lean ground turkey

- 1 small yellow bell pepper, seeded and chopped finely

- 1 small red bell pepper, seeded and chopped finely

- Salt and freshly ground black pepper, to taste

Directions:

1. Put all the ingredients in a large bowl and mix until well combined.

2. Make 24 balls equal-sized from mixture.

3. Heat oil in a skillet over medium heat and add meatballs.

4. Cook for about 6 minutes until golden brown on all sides.

5. Cover the skillet and cook for about 5 more minutes.

6. Place 3 meatballs on each plate and serve hot.

Nutritional Value:

Calories 190

Total Fat 6.1 g

Saturated Fat 1.3 g

Cholesterol 53 mg

Sodium 52 mg

Total Carbs 17.6 g

Fiber 4.2 g

Sugar 2 g

Protein 17.8 g

Potassium 436 mg

Beef Sirloin Steak

Servings: 6

Prep Time: 10 minutes

Cooking Time: 30 minutes

Total Time: 40 minutes

Ingredients:

- 2 pounds beef top sirloin steaks

- 1 teaspoon garlic powder

- 2 garlic cloves, minced

- ¼ cup tea seed oil

- Salt and freshly ground black pepper, to taste

Directions:

1. Melt tea seed oil in a large grill pan and add beef sirloin steaks.

2. Brown the steaks on both sides by cooking for 2 minutes on each side.

3. Add the remaining ingredients and cook for 12 minutes on each side on medium-high heat.

4. Dish out the juicy steaks onto a serving platter and serve with a baked potato.

Nutritional Information:

Calories 246

Total Fat 13.1 g

Saturated Fat 7.6 g

Cholesterol 81 mg

Sodium 224 mg

Total Carbs 2 g

Sugar 0.1 g

Fiber 0.1 g

Potassium 11 mg

Protein 31.3 g

GLOW 15 LOW-DAY

RECIPES

Broccoli Avocado Salad

Servings: 2

Preparation Time: 5 minutes

Cooking Time: 0 minutes

Total Time: 5 minutes

Ingredients:

- 1 head broccoli, chopped

- 2 tablespoons tea seed oil

- 2 tablespoons pomegranate seeds

- ¼ cup almonds, chopped

- 1 avocado, chopped

- 2 teaspoons lemon juice

- 2 teaspoons fresh oregano

- Salt, to taste

Directions:

1. Mix together broccoli, avocado, pomegranate seeds and almonds in a medium bowl.

2. Whisk together tea seed oil, fresh oregano and lemon juice and season with salt.

3. Drizzle the oil mixture over the broccoli mixture and toss to coat well.

4. Dish out into a serving bowl and serve immediately.

Nutritional Value:

Calories 358

Total Fat 32.6 g

Saturated Fat 3.9 g

Cholesterol 0 mg

Sodium 23 mg

Total Carbs 15 g

Fiber 9.3 g

Sugar 2.1 g

Protein 5.7 g

Potassium 701 mg

Spinach and Fruits Salad

Servings: 3

Preparation Time: 10 minutes

Cooking Time: 0 minutes

Total Time: 10 minutes

Ingredients:

- 1 grapefruit, peeled and sectioned

- 1 mango, peeled, pitted and cubed

- 1 avocado, chopped

- 3 tablespoons fresh lime juice

- ¼ cup fresh mint leaves, chopped

- 3 cups fresh baby spinach

Directions:

1. Mix together all the ingredients in a large serving bowl except spinach.

2. Toss to coat well and refrigerate to chill before serving.

3. Divide spinach onto serving plates and top with salad evenly before serving.

4. Serve immediately.

Nutritional Value:

Calories 229

Total Fat 13.7 g

Saturated Fat 2.9 g

Cholesterol 0 mg

Sodium 31 mg

Total Carbs 28.3 g

Fiber 8 g

Sugar 18.9 g

Protein 3.6 g

Potassium 782 mg

Asparagus Soup

Servings: 4

Preparation Time: 15 minutes

Cooking Time: 8 minutes

Total Time: 23 minutes

Ingredients:

- 1 tablespoon tea seed oil

- 3 scallions, chopped

- 1 avocado, sliced

- 1 pound asparagus, trimmed and chopped

- 4 cups vegetable broth

- 2 tablespoons fresh lemon juice

- Salt and freshly ground black pepper, to taste

Directions:

1. Heat oil in a large pan over medium heat and sauté scallions for about 5 minutes.

2. Put the asparagus, scallions, avocado, broth, salt and pepper in an immersion blender and blend until smooth.

3. Put the mixture into a pot and simmer for about 3 minutes on medium heat.

4. Top with avocado slices and dish out in serving bowls.

5. Serve simmering hot to your guests and let them enjoy.

Nutritional Value:

Calories 199

Total Fat 14.6 g

Saturated Fat 2.9 g

Cholesterol 0 mg

Sodium 772 mg

Total Carbs 10.6 g

Fiber 6.1 g

Sugar 3.5 g

Protein 8.6 g

Potassium 720 mg

Grilled Veggies

Servings: 4

Preparation Time: 15 minutes

Cooking Time: 8 minutes

Total Time: 23 minutes

Ingredients:

- ¼ cup tea seed oil

- 2 tablespoons raw honey

- ½ teaspoon garlic powder

- 1 medium yellow squash, cut into ½-inch slices

- 1 large red bell pepper seeded and cut into 1-inch strips

- 4 teaspoons balsamic vinegar

- 1 teaspoon dried oregano, crushed

- 1 teaspoon ground cumin

- Salt and freshly ground black pepper, to taste

- 3 small carrots, peeled and halved lengthwise

- 1 pound fresh asparagus, trimmed

- 1 medium red onion, cut into wedges

Directions:

1. Mix together all the ingredients in a small bowl except vegetables.

2. Put 3 tablespoons of marinade in a large bowl, reserving the remaining.

3. Add vegetables to the marinade and toss to coat well.

4. Keep aside, covered for about 2 hours.

5. Preheat the grill to medium heat and grease the grill grate.

6. Place the vegetables over grill grate in a single layer and grill, covered for about 12 minutes, occasionally flipping.

7. Drizzle the reserved marinade on the grilled vegetables and dish out on a serving platter.

Nutritional Value:

Calories 111

Total Fat 1.3 g

Saturated Fat 0.2 g

Cholesterol 0 mg

Sodium 37 mg

Total Carbs 24 g

Fiber 5.1 g

Sugar 16.3 g

Protein 4.2 g

Potassium 602 mg

Salt and Vinegar Bok Choy

Servings: 6

Preparation Time: 15 minutes

Cooking Time: 15 minutes

Total Time: 30 minutes

Ingredients:

- 2 pounds bok choy

- 3 tablespoons tea seed oil

- 1 teaspoon ginger powder

- 3 tablespoons apple cider vinegar

- Coarse salt, to taste

Directions:

1. Wash and dry the bok choy well.

2. Preheat the oven to 350 degrees F and line a

baking sheet with parchment paper.

3. Mix together bok choy, tea seed oil, ginger powder, apple cider vinegar and salt in a large bowl.

4. Massage the bok choy with clean hands for 2 minutes to help break it down a bit.

5. Spread the bok choy into a single layer on the prepared baking sheet.

6. Bake for 5 minutes, keeping an eye on the bok choy, so it doesn't burn.

7. Toss with a wooden spoon or a spatula and bake for 10 more minutes, until browned and crispy around the edges.

8. Dish out and serve hot.

Nutritional Value:

Calories 82

Total Fat 6.8 g

Saturated Fat 0.8 g

Cholesterol 0 mg

Sodium 99 mg

Total Carbs 3.6 g

Fiber 1.6 g

Sugar 1.8 g

Protein 2.3 g

Potassium 391 mg

Herbed Green Smoothie

Servings: 2

Preparation Time: 10 minutes

Cooking Time: 0 minutes

Total Time: 10 minutes

Ingredients:

- 1 small cucumber, peeled and chopped

- ¼ cup fresh parsley leaves

- 1½ tablespoons honey

- 1½ cups chilled water

- 2 cups mixed fresh greens (spinach, kale, beet greens), trimmed and chopped

- ½ cup lettuce, torn

- ¼ cup fresh mint leaves

- 1 tablespoon fresh lemon juice

Directions:

1. Put cucumber, fresh parsley leaves, honey, mixed fresh greens, lettuce, fresh mint leaves, lemon juice and chilled water in a high-speed blender and pulse until smooth.

2. Pour into 2 glasses and immediately serve.

Nutritional Value:

Calories 115

Total Fat 0.4 g

Saturated Fat 0.2 g

Cholesterol 0 mg

Sodium 43 mg

Total Carbs 27.4 g

Fiber 2.9 g

Sugar 15.8 g

Protein 3.8 g

Potassium 681 mg

Miso-Glazed Brussels Sprouts

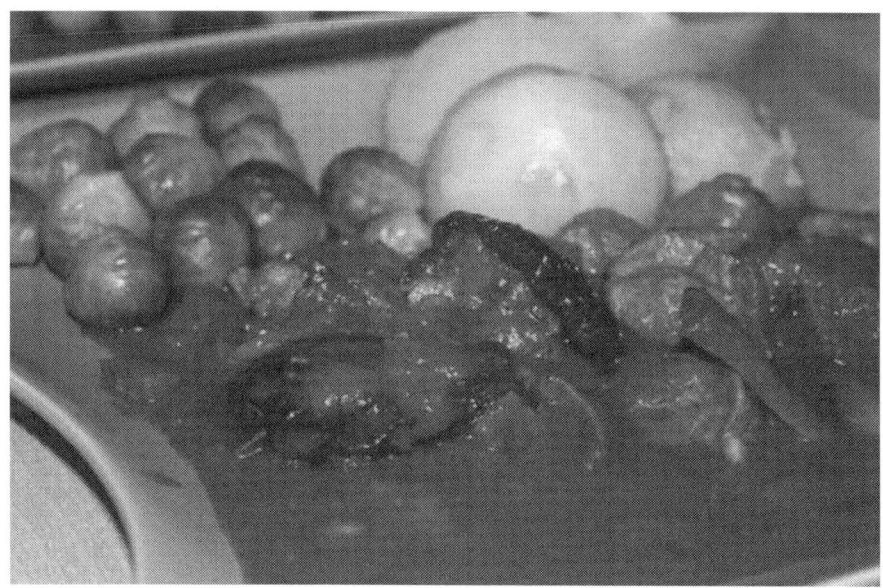

Servings: 2

Preparation Time: 5 minutes

Cooking Time: 15 minutes

Total Time: 20 minutes

Ingredients:

- 1½ teaspoons mirin

- 2 teaspoons dark sesame oil

- 1 tablespoon sesame seeds

- 1½ tablespoons miso paste

- ½ pound Brussels sprouts

- 1 tablespoon fresh basil, chopped

- ¼ cup kimchi

Directions:

1. Preheat the oven to 400 degrees F and grease a baking dish.

2. Whisk together mirin, miso and 2 tablespoons water in a small bowl until well combined.

3. Brush the Brussels sprouts with dark sesame oil and roast for 10 minutes until golden brown.

4. Dish out the Brussels sprouts on a serving platter and sprinkle with basil and sesame seeds.

5. Drizzle with mirin mixture and serve with kimchi on the side.

Nutritional Value:

Calories 149

Total Fat 7.9 g

Saturated Fat 1.2 g

Cholesterol 0 mg

Sodium 584 mg

Total Carbs 16.8 g

Fiber 5.5 g

Sugar 4.3 g

Protein 6.2 g

Potassium 493 mg

Citrus Carrots

Servings: 4

Preparation Time: 15 minutes

Cooking Time: 5 minutes

Total Time: 20 minutes

Ingredients:

- 2 teaspoons tea seed oil

- 2 teaspoons fresh ginger, minced

- 3 cups carrots, peeled and grated

- ½ cup fresh orange juice

- Salt and freshly ground black pepper, to taste

Directions:

1. Heat oil in a large non-stick skillet over medium-high heat and add carrots and ginger.

2. Cook for about 2 minutes, occasionally stirring and reduce the heat to low.

3. Stir in orange juice, salt and black pepper and simmer for about 2 minutes.

4. Dish out On a serving platter and serve hot.

Nutritional Value:

Calories 111

Total Fat 6.6 g

Saturated Fat 0.8 g

Cholesterol 0 mg

Sodium 57 mg

Total Carbs 12 g

Fiber 2.2 g

Sugar 6.7 g

Protein 1 g

Potassium 338 mg

Berries and Dandelion Smoothie

Servings: 2

Preparation Time: 10 minutes

Cooking Time: 0 minutes

Total Time: 10 minutes

Ingredients:

- 1 cup frozen mixed berries

- 2 cups fresh dandelion greens

- 1½ cups unsweetened almond milk

- 1 frozen banana, peeled and sliced

- 2 tablespoons flaxseeds

- ¼ cup ice cubes, crushed

Directions:

1. Put the frozen mixed berries, fresh dandelion greens, unsweetened almond milk, frozen banana, flaxseeds and ice cubes in a high-speed blender and pulse until smooth.

2. Pour into 2 glasses and immediately serve.

Nutritional Value:

Calories 160

Total Fat 6.2 g

Saturated Fat 1.1 g

Cholesterol 2 mg

Sodium 188 mg

Total Carbs 22.2 g

Fiber 0.9 g

Sugar 2.3 g

Protein 10 g

Potassium 128 mg

Sautéed Cauliflower

Servings: 4

Preparation Time: 10 minutes

Cooking Time: 10 minutes

Total Time: 20 minutes

Ingredients:

- 1 head cauliflower, trimmed and cut into bite-size

  pieces

- 3 tablespoons tea seed oil

- ½ teaspoon salt

- 1 tablespoon fresh lemon juice

- 1 large avocado, sliced

- 3 garlic cloves, chopped

- ½ cup vegetable broth

- 1 teaspoon lemon zest

- ½ cup broccoli sprouts

Directions:

1. Heat the oil in a large skillet over medium heat and add garlic.

2. Cook for about 30 seconds, stirring continuously.

3. Stir in the cauliflower and cook for about 3 minutes.

4. Add the broth, salt, lemon zest and lemon juice and cook for about 5 minutes.

5. Top with the broccoli sprouts and avocado and serve immediately.

Nutritional Value:

Calories 226

Total Fat 19.9 g

Saturated Fat 3.3 g

Cholesterol 0 mg

Sodium 414 mg

Total Carbs 10.9 g

Fiber 5.8 g

Sugar 2.6 g

Protein 3.5 g

Potassium 540 mg

Roasted Tomatoes

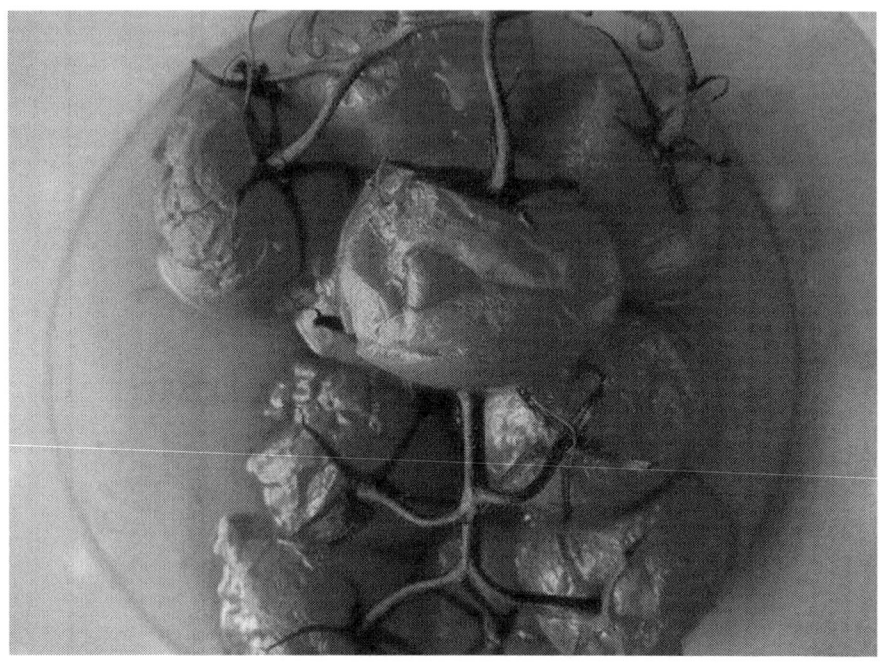

Servings: 6

Preparation Time: 10 minutes

Cooking Time: 20 minutes

Total Time: 30 minutes

Ingredients:

- 6 large tomatoes, halved

- 2 tablespoons onion, chopped finely

- 1 jalapeño pepper, seeded and minced

- 1 teaspoon fresh thyme, minced

- Freshly ground black pepper, to taste

- 4 cups fresh baby spinach

- Salt, to taste

- 3 garlic cloves, minced

- 1 tablespoon fresh rosemary, minced

- 1 teaspoon fresh oregano, minced

- 2 tablespoons tea seed oil

Directions:

1. Sprinkle the tomatoes with a little salt and arrange tomatoes onto paper towel lined plate, cut side down.

2. Keep aside for about 40 minutes to completely drain.

3. Preheat the oven to 425 degrees F and grease a baking dish.

4. Mix together onion, garlic, jalapeño pepper, herbs and black pepper in a small bowl.

5. Place tomatoes in prepared baking dish in a single layer, cut side up.

6. Top each tomato piece evenly with herb mixture and drizzle generously with tea seed oil.

7. Roast for about 20 minutes and serve hot.

Nutritional Value:

Calories 85

Total Fat 4.9 g

Saturated Fat 0.6 g

Cholesterol 0 mg

Sodium 53 mg

Total Carbs 9.4 g

Fiber 3.2 g

Sugar 5.1 g

Protein 2.4 g

Potassium 570 mg

GLOW 15

AUTOPHASAUCES RECIPES

Special Avocado Dip

Servings: 8

Preparation Time: 5 minutes

Cooking Time: 0 minutes

Total Time: 5 minutes

Ingredients:

- ½ small avocado

- 2 tablespoons raw apple cider vinegar

- ¼ cup fresh parsley

- 1/8 cup fresh mint

- 1 teaspoon dulse flakes

- ¼ cup tea seed oil

- ¼ cup fresh basil

- 1 teaspoon trehalose

- Salt and black pepper, to taste

Directions:

1. Put avocado, raw apple cider vinegar, fresh

parsley, fresh mint, dulse flakes, tea seed oil, fresh

basil, trehalose, salt and black pepper in a food processor and process until smooth.

2. Dish out into a serving bowl and serve with snacks.

Nutritional Value:

Calories 35

Total Fat 2.9 g

Saturated Fat 0.6 g

Cholesterol 0 mg

Sodium 4 mg

Total Carbs 2.1 g

Fiber 1 g

Sugar 0.8 g

Protein 0.4 g

Potassium 94 mg

Black Beans Dip

Servings: 6

Preparation Time: 5 minutes

Cooking Time: 15 minutes

Total Time: 20 minutes

Ingredients:

- 1 cup black beans, soaked overnight

- 2 cups water

- 1 small onion, chopped

- 3 cloves garlic

- 1 tablespoon tea seed oil

- 14 oz. canned tomatoes in their juice

- 1 teaspoon chili powder

- ½ teaspoon dried oregano

- 1 cup cottage cheese, shredded

- Salt and black pepper, to taste

Directions:

1. Put black beans, water, onion, garlic, tea seed oil, tomatoes, chili powder, dried oregano, cottage cheese, salt and black pepper in the cooker pot and lock the lid.

2. Cook on high pressure for 15 minutes and release the pressure naturally.

3. Put the contents of the cooker pot in a blender and blend until smooth.

4. Dish out the dip into a bowl and garnish with cilantro, salt and black pepper.

Nutritional Value:

Calories 205

Total Fat 3.6 g

Saturated Fat 0.8 g

Cholesterol 3 mg

Sodium 401 mg

Total Carbs 30.7 g

Fiber 5.7 g

Sugar 3.6 g

Protein 12.9 g

Potassium 609 mg

Spinach Dip

Servings: 11

Preparation Time: 20 minutes

Cooking Time: 30 minutes

Total Time: 50 minutes

Ingredients:

- 7-ounce artichoke hearts, drained and chopped

- ¼ cup fat-free sour cream

- ½ (10-ounce) bag frozen chopped spinach, thawed, drained and squeezed

- 1½ garlic cloves, minced

- 1 (8-ounce) package fat-free cream cheese, softened

- 1/8 cup Pecorino Romano cheese, grated freshly and divided

- Salt and freshly ground black pepper, to taste

- ¾ cup part-skim mozzarella cheese, shredded and divided

Directions:

1. Preheat the oven to 350 degrees F and grease a baking dish with cooking spray.

2. Mix together artichokes, spinach, garlic, sour cream, cream cheese, salt, black pepper, 2

tablespoons of Pecorino Romano cheese and ½ cup of mozzarella cheese in a baking dish.

3. Mix together remaining cheeses in a small bowl and sprinkle the cheese mixture on top of spinach mixture.

4. Bake for about 30 minutes until bubbly.

5. Preheat the broiler and set the oven to broil.

6. Broil the dip for about 3 minutes and serve warm.

Nutritional Value:

Calories 94

Total Fat 7.7 g

Saturated Fat 4.8 g

Cholesterol 25 mg

Sodium 103 mg

Total Carbs 3.7 g

Fiber 1 g

Sugar 0.6 g

Protein 3.1 g

Potassium 93 mg

Parsley and Basil Dip

Servings: 8

Preparation Time: 5 minutes

Cooking Time: 0 minutes

Total Time: 5 minutes

Ingredients:

- 3-ounces fresh basil, stems removed

- ½ cup tea seed oil

- ¼ cup coconut aminos

- 1 large bunch parsley, ends trimmed

- ½ lime, juiced

- ½ teaspoon lime zest

Directions:

1. Put fresh basil, tea seed oil, coconut aminos, parsley, lime juice and zest in a food processor and process until smooth.

2. Dish out into a bowl and serve with snacks.

3. Store in an airtight container in the refrigerator for about 1 week.

Nutritional Value:

Calories 21

Total Fat 1 g

Saturated Fat 0.1 g

Cholesterol 0 mg

Sodium 13 mg

Total Carbs 2.7 g

Fiber 0.6 g

Sugar 0.2 g

Protein 0.6 g

Potassium 77 mg

Olives and Cherry Tomatoes Dip

Servings: 8

Preparation Time: 5 minutes

Cooking Time: 0 minutes

Total Time: 5 minutes

Ingredients:

- 1 cup macadamia nuts

- ¼ cup black olives, pitted and oil-cured

- ¼ teaspoon salt

- ½ cup fresh parsley, chopped

- ½ cup cherry tomatoes

- ½ lemon, juiced

- Freshly ground black pepper, to taste

Directions:

1. Put macadamia nuts with rest of the ingredients in the blender and blend until smooth.

2. Dish out into a serving bowl and serve with snacks.

3. Store in an airtight container in the refrigerator for about 1 week.

Nutritional Value:

Calories 130

Total Fat 13.2 g

Saturated Fat 2.1 g

Cholesterol 0 mg

Sodium 114 mg

Total Carbs 3.6 g

Fiber 1.9 g

Sugar 1.2 g

Protein 1.6 g

Potassium 114 mg

Maple-Scented Tahini Dip

Servings: 8

Preparation Time: 5 minutes

Cooking Time: 0 minutes

Total Time: 5 minutes

Ingredients:

- 1 tablespoon tea seed oil

- 1 lemon, juiced

- ½ teaspoon salt

- 2/3 cup tahini

- 2 teaspoons pure maple syrup

- 2 small garlic cloves

- ¼ teaspoon freshly ground black pepper

Directions:

1. Mix together all the ingredients in a food processor and add ½ cup water.

2. Process until smooth and dish out into a bowl.

3. Store in an airtight container in the refrigerator for up to 1 week.

Nutritional Value:

Calories 142

Total Fat 12.4 g

Saturated Fat 1.7 g

Cholesterol 0 mg

Sodium 171 mg

Total Carbs 6.3 g

Fiber 2.1 g

Sugar 1.3 g

Protein 3.5 g

Potassium 99 mg

Miso Almond Dip

Servings: 16

Preparation Time: 5 minutes

Cooking Time: 0 minutes

Total Time: 5 minutes

Ingredients:

- 4 tablespoons white miso paste

- 2 tablespoons coconut aminos

- ½ teaspoon salt

- ½ cup fresh cilantro, chopped

- 1 cup almond butter, unsweetened

- 1 cup carrots, grated

- 1 lime, juiced

- 2 (1-inch) pieces fresh ginger, peeled and grated

- ¼ teaspoon freshly ground black pepper

Directions:

1. Put white miso paste, coconut aminos, salt, fresh cilantro, almond butter, carrots, lime juice, fresh ginger and black pepper in an immersion blender and add ½ cup water.

2. Blend until smooth and dish out into a bowl.

3. Store in an airtight container in the refrigerator for up to 1 week.

Nutritional Value:

Calories 22

Total Fat 0.8 g

Saturated Fat 0 g

Cholesterol 0 mg

Sodium 278 mg

Total Carbs 2.9 g

Fiber 0.4 g

Sugar 0.5 g

Protein 0.8 g

Potassium 40 mg

Greens Pesto

Servings: 9

Preparation Time: 5 minutes

Cooking Time: 0 minutes

Total Time: 5 minutes

Ingredients:

- ¼ cup spinach

- 2 tablespoons fresh thyme leaves

- 4 garlic cloves, coarsely chopped

- ½ avocado

- 1 lemon, juiced

- 1 bunch parsley, ends trimmed

- 2 teaspoons fresh rosemary leaves

- ½ cup tea seed oil

- Sea salt, to taste

Directions:

1. Combine all the ingredients in an immersion blender and close the lid.

2. Blend until smooth and dish out into a bowl.

3. You can store in an airtight container in the refrigerator for up to 1 week.

Nutritional Value:

Calories 38

Total Fat 3.1 g

Saturated Fat 0.6 g

Cholesterol 0 mg

Sodium 6 mg

Total Carbs 3 g

Fiber 1.5 g

Sugar 0.3 g

Protein 0.6 g

Potassium 117 mg

Avocado Cheese Dip

Servings: 9

Preparation Time: 5 minutes

Cooking Time: 0 minutes

Total Time: 5 minutes

Ingredients:

- 2 large avocado, seeds removed

- 10 oz. Pecorino Romano cheese

- 16 oz. cream cheese

- ½ tablespoon garlic, minced

- 1 teaspoon onion powder

Directions:

1. Put the avocado, cream cheese and Pecorino Romano cheese in the food processor.

2. Process until creamy and well combined.

3. Mix well while still in the food processor and add minced garlic and onion powder.

4. Process until well combined and serve with snacks.

Nutritional Value:

Calories 332

Total Fat 29 g

Saturated Fat 16.9 g

Cholesterol 88 mg

Sodium 529 mg

Total Carbs 4.5 g

Fiber 1.3 g

Sugar 0.5 g

Protein 14.3 g

Potassium 189 mg

Yogurt Dip

Servings: 9

Preparation Time: 5 minutes

Cooking Time: 0 minutes

Total Time: 5 minutes

Ingredients:

- 1 cup low-fat yogurt

- 1 tablespoon fresh mint, chopped

- 1 tablespoon honey

- 2 tablespoons fresh lemon juice

- 1 tablespoon fresh cilantro, chopped

- ½ teaspoon salt

- ¼ teaspoon black pepper

- 1 red chili, for topping

Directions:

1. Mix together yogurt, lemon juice, honey, mint, cilantro, ½ teaspoon salt and ¼ teaspoon pepper in a bowl.

2. Season with additional salt and pepper if required and top with red chili.

Nutritional Value:

Calories 28

Total Fat 0.4 g

Saturated Fat 0.3 g

Cholesterol 2 mg

Sodium 148 mg

Total Carbs 4 g

Fiber 0.1 g

Sugar 3.9 g

Protein 1.6 g

Potassium 73 mg

GLOW 15 Recipe Book

Grocery List:

Shrimp Lettuce Wraps

Ingredients:

- 1 pound shrimps

- 2 tablespoons olive oil

- 2 garlic cloves, minced

- 1 green bell pepper, seeded and chopped

- ½ cup summer squash, chopped

- ½ teaspoon curry powder

- 1 onion, chopped

- 1 cup carrot, peeled and chopped

- ½ cup zucchini, chopped

- 2 tablespoons low-sodium soy sauce

- Freshly ground black pepper, to taste

- 10 large lettuce leaves

Crunchy Chicken

Ingredients:

- 8 skinless, boneless chicken tenderloins

- 2 tablespoons tea seed oil

- 2 tablespoons low-fat yogurt

- 1 teaspoon turmeric powder

- Salt and freshly ground black pepper, to taste

Turkey Salad

Ingredients:

- 5 ounce turkey meat, cooked

- 2 tablespoons tahini

- ¼ cup celery, chopped

- 2 tablespoons avocado mayonnaise

- ½ lemon, juiced

- ½ teaspoon ground turmeric

- 1 cup broccoli sprouts

- Freshly ground pepper, to taste

Delicious Whole Chicken

Ingredients:

- ½ tablespoon fresh rosemary, minced

- 1 teaspoon ground cumin

- 1 teaspoon cayenne pepper

- 1 teaspoon red pepper flakes, crushed

- Salt and freshly ground black pepper, to taste

- 1 pound organic whole chicken, neck and giblet removed

- 1 tablespoon tea seed oil

Stir Fried Broccoli and Salmon

Ingredients:

- 1 pound salmon, chunked

- 2 garlic cloves, minced

- 1 tablespoon gluten free coconut aminos

- 1 tablespoon dark sesame oil

- 5 cups broccoli, chopped

- ¾ teaspoon red pepper flakes

- 3 scallions, thinly sliced

- 1-inch piece fresh ginger, minced

- 3 tablespoons tea seed oil

- Salt and freshly ground black pepper, to taste

- 2 tablespoons sesame seeds

Chicken Stew

Ingredients:

- 1 tablespoon tea seed oil

- 1 pound fresh mushrooms, stemmed and quartered

- 1 small yellow onion, chopped

- 1 tablespoon sugar-free tomato paste

- 3 garlic cloves, minced

- 6 (5-ounce) grass-fed skinless, boneless chicken thighs

- 1 cup green olives, pitted and halved

- 2 cups fresh cherry tomatoes, halved

- 1 cup homemade chicken broth

- ½ cup water

- Salt and freshly ground black pepper, to taste

- ¼ cup fresh parsley, chopped

Beef with Mixed Herb Butter

Ingredients:

- 4 (6-ounce) beef steaks

- 1 lemon, halved

- 2 teaspoons fresh dill, chopped

- 2½ tablespoons unsalted butter

- 2 teaspoons fresh thyme

- 2 garlic cloves, minced

- Salt and freshly ground black pepper, to taste

Pork and Beans Chili

Ingredients:

- 2 pounds grass-fed pork, ground

- 2 garlic cloves, minced

- 3 teaspoons red chili powder

- 1 (15-ounce) can black beans, rinsed and drained

- 3 cups fresh baby spinach

- 6-ounce tomato paste

- 1 tablespoon tea seed oil

- ¼ cup onion, chopped

- 1 teaspoon fresh ginger, minced

- 1 teaspoon dried thyme

- 1 teaspoon ground cumin

- 3 tomatoes, chopped

- 1 cup water

Broiled Tilapia

Ingredients:

- ½ cup Pecorino Romano cheese, grated

- 2 tablespoons avocado mayonnaise

- 2 tablespoons tea seed oil

- 2 tablespoons fresh lemon juice

- 2 pounds tilapia fillets

- ¼ teaspoon dried thyme

- Salt and freshly ground black pepper, to taste

Turkey Meatballs

Ingredients:

- 1 cup cooked black beans, mashed roughly

- ½ cup fresh parsley, chopped

- Tea seed oil, as required

- 1 pound extra-lean ground turkey

- 1 small yellow bell pepper, seeded and chopped finely

- 1 small red bell pepper, seeded and chopped finely

- Salt and freshly ground black pepper, to taste

Beef Sirloin Steak

Ingredients:

- 2 pounds beef top sirloin steaks

- 1 teaspoon garlic powder

- 2 garlic cloves, minced

- ¼ cup tea seed oil

- Salt and freshly ground black pepper, to taste

Broccoli Avocado Salad

Ingredients:

- 1 head broccoli, chopped

- 2 tablespoons tea seed oil

- 2 tablespoons pomegranate seeds

- ¼ cup almonds, chopped

- 1 avocado, chopped

- 2 teaspoons lemon juice

- 2 teaspoons fresh oregano

- Salt, to taste

Spinach and Fruits Salad

Ingredients:

- 1 grapefruit, peeled and sectioned

- 1 mango, peeled, pitted and cubed

- 1 avocado, chopped

- 3 tablespoons fresh lime juice

- ¼ cup fresh mint leaves, chopped

- 3 cups fresh baby spinach

Asparagus Soup

Ingredients:

- 1 tablespoon tea seed oil

- 3 scallions, chopped

- 1 avocado, sliced

- 1 pound asparagus, trimmed and chopped

- 4 cups vegetable broth

- 2 tablespoons fresh lemon juice

- Salt and freshly ground black pepper, to taste

Grilled Veggies

Ingredients:

- ¼ cup tea seed oil

- 2 tablespoons raw honey

- ½ teaspoon garlic powder

- 1 medium yellow squash, cut into ½-inch slices

- 1 large red bell pepper seeded and cut into 1-inch strips
- 4 teaspoons balsamic vinegar
- 1 teaspoon dried oregano, crushed
- 1 teaspoon ground cumin
- Salt and freshly ground black pepper, to taste
- 3 small carrots, peeled and halved lengthwise
- 1 pound fresh asparagus, trimmed
- 1 medium red onion, cut into wedges

Salt and Vinegar Bok Choy

Ingredients:

- 2 pounds bok choy

- 3 tablespoons tea seed oil

- 1 teaspoon ginger powder

- 3 tablespoons apple cider vinegar

- Coarse salt, to taste

Herbed Green Smoothie

Ingredients:

- 1 small cucumber, peeled and chopped

- ¼ cup fresh parsley leaves

- 1½ tablespoons honey

- 1½ cups chilled water

- 2 cups mixed fresh greens (spinach, kale, beet greens), trimmed and chopped

- ½ cup lettuce, torn

- ¼ cup fresh mint leaves

- 1 tablespoon fresh lemon juice

Miso-Glazed Brussels Sprouts

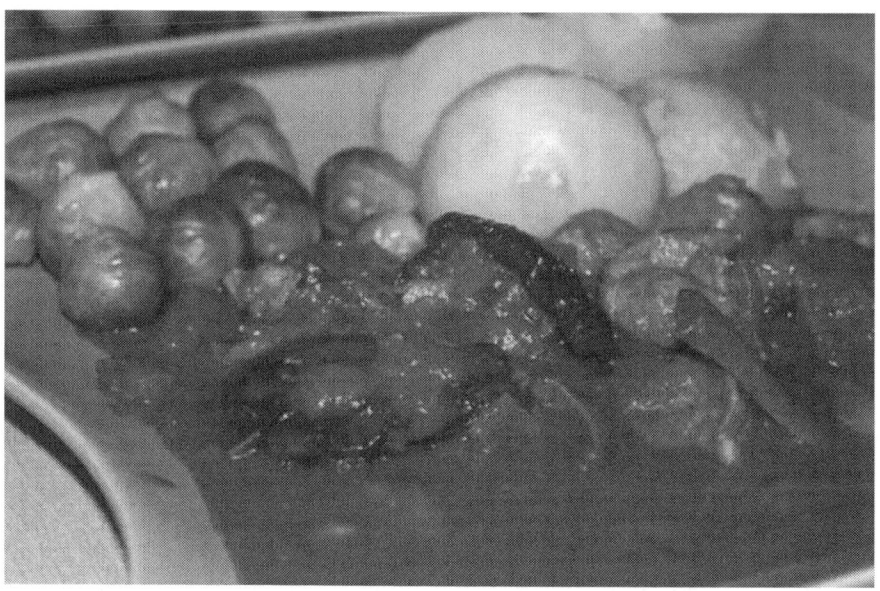

Ingredients:

- 1½ teaspoons mirin

- 2 teaspoons dark sesame oil

- 1 tablespoon sesame seeds

- 1½ tablespoons miso paste

- ½ pound Brussels sprouts

- 1 tablespoon fresh basil, chopped

- ¼ cup kimchi

Citrus Carrots

Ingredients:

- 2 teaspoons tea seed oil

- 2 teaspoons fresh ginger, minced

- 3 cups carrots, peeled and grated

- ½ cup fresh orange juice

- Salt and freshly ground black pepper, to taste

Berries and Dandelion Smoothie

Ingredients:

- 1 cup frozen mixed berries

- 2 cups fresh dandelion greens

- 1½ cups unsweetened almond milk

- 1 frozen banana, peeled and sliced

- 2 tablespoons flaxseeds

- ¼ cup ice cubes, crushed

Sautéed Cauliflower

Ingredients:

- 1 head cauliflower, trimmed and cut into bite-size

  pieces

- 3 tablespoons tea seed oil

- ½ teaspoon salt

- 1 tablespoon fresh lemon juice

- 1 large avocado, sliced

- 3 garlic cloves, chopped

- ½ cup vegetable broth

- 1 teaspoon lemon zest

- ½ cup broccoli sprouts

Roasted Tomatoes

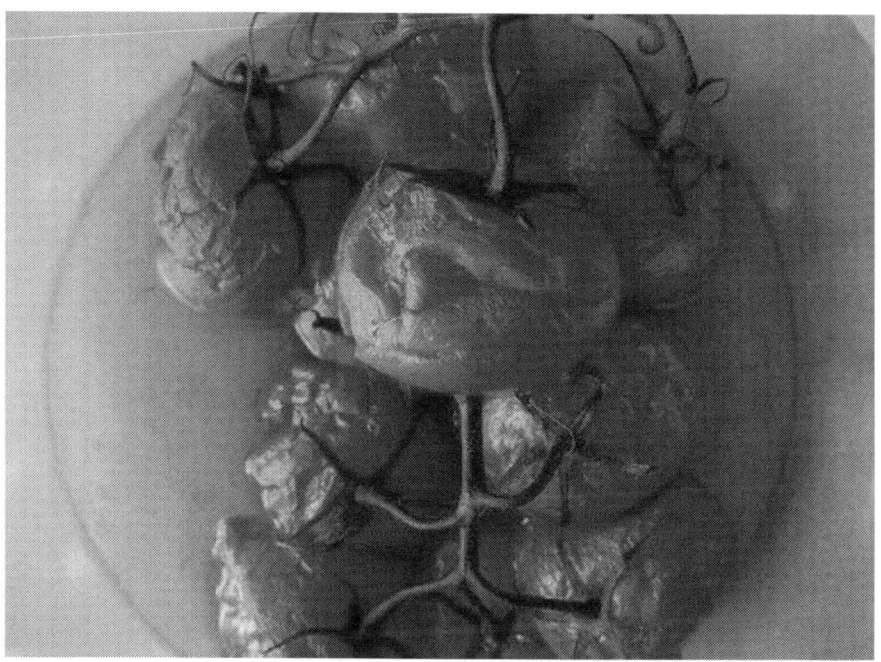

Ingredients:

- 6 large tomatoes, halved

- 2 tablespoons onion, chopped finely

- 1 jalapeño pepper, seeded and minced

- 1 teaspoon fresh thyme, minced

- Freshly ground black pepper, to taste

- 4 cups fresh baby spinach

- Salt, to taste

- 3 garlic cloves, minced

- 1 tablespoon fresh rosemary, minced

- 1 teaspoon fresh oregano, minced

- 2 tablespoons tea seed oil

Special Avocado Dip

Ingredients:

- ½ small avocado

- 2 tablespoons raw apple cider vinegar

- ¼ cup fresh parsley

- 1/8 cup fresh mint

- 1 teaspoon dulse flakes

- ¼ cup tea seed oil

- ¼ cup fresh basil

- 1 teaspoon trehalose

- Salt and black pepper, to taste

Black Beans Dip

Ingredients:

- 1 cup black beans, soaked overnight

- 2 cups water

- 1 small onion, chopped

- 3 cloves garlic

- 1 tablespoon tea seed oil

- 14 oz. canned tomatoes in their juice

- 1 teaspoon chili powder

- ½ teaspoon dried oregano

- 1 cup cottage cheese, shredded

- Salt and black pepper, to taste

Spinach Dip

Ingredients:

- 7-ounce artichoke hearts, drained and chopped

- ¼ cup fat-free sour cream

- ½ (10-ounce) bag frozen chopped spinach, thawed, drained and squeezed

- 1½ garlic cloves, minced

- 1 (8-ounce) package fat-free cream cheese, softened

- 1/8 cup Pecorino Romano cheese, grated freshly and divided

- Salt and freshly ground black pepper, to taste

- ¾ cup part-skim mozzarella cheese, shredded and divided

Parsley and Basil Dip

Ingredients:

- 3-ounces fresh basil, stems removed

- ½ cup tea seed oil

- ¼ cup coconut aminos

- 1 large bunch parsley, ends trimmed

- ½ lime, juiced

- ½ teaspoon lime zest

Olives and Cherry Tomatoes Dip

Ingredients:

- 1 cup macadamia nuts

- ¼ cup black olives, pitted and oil-cured

- ¼ teaspoon salt

- ½ cup fresh parsley, chopped

- ½ cup cherry tomatoes

- ½ lemon, juiced

- Freshly ground black pepper, to taste

Maple-Scented Tahini Dip

Ingredients:

- 1 tablespoon tea seed oil

- 1 lemon, juiced

- ½ teaspoon salt

- 2/3 cup tahini

- 2 teaspoons pure maple syrup

- 2 small garlic cloves

- ¼ teaspoon freshly ground black pepper

Miso Almond Dip

Ingredients:

- 4 tablespoons white miso paste

- 2 tablespoons coconut aminos

- ½ teaspoon salt

- ½ cup fresh cilantro, chopped

- 1 cup almond butter, unsweetened

- 1 cup carrots, grated

- 1 lime, juiced

- 2 (1-inch) pieces fresh ginger, peeled and grated

- ¼ teaspoon freshly ground black pepper

Greens Pesto

Ingredients:

- ¼ cup spinach

- 2 tablespoons fresh thyme leaves

- 4 garlic cloves, coarsely chopped

- ½ avocado

- 1 lemon, juiced

- 1 bunch parsley, ends trimmed

- 2 teaspoons fresh rosemary leaves

- ½ cup tea seed oil

- Sea salt, to taste

Avocado Cheese Dip

Ingredients:

- 2 large avocado, seeds removed

- 10 oz. Pecorino Romano cheese

- 16 oz. cream cheese

- ½ tablespoon garlic, minced

- 1 teaspoon onion powder

Yogurt Dip

Ingredients:

- 1 cup low-fat yogurt

- 1 tablespoon fresh mint, chopped

- 1 tablespoon honey

- 2 tablespoons fresh lemon juice

- 1 tablespoon fresh cilantro, chopped

- ½ teaspoon salt

- ¼ teaspoon black pepper

- 1 red chili, for topping

Grab Your Free Bonus Now

Thank you for purchasing this book! You can get your free gift here:

Free Special Recipes Collection

Download It Immediately Here:

http://cookbooks247.com/bonus

FINAL SURPRISE BONUS

Did you enjoy the cookbook?

We hope you enjoyed it as much as we did delivering it to you.

We are passionate about cooking and crafting unique, delicious recipes.

If you've enjoyed the book, can you do us a small favor and leave a review so it can reach more readers?

If you do, I'll send you a "special surprise bonus"

5 More Tantalizing Recipes on Glow 15 Unofficial Recipe Book by Karah Westlake

Here's how to claim your free report:

1. Leave a review (longer the better but I'd be grateful for whatever length) at the bookstore you've purchased it from (Amazon, iBooks, Kobo, etc)

2. Send a screenshot of your posted review here: mycookbook247@gmail.com

3. your bonus within 24-48 hours!

Receive your free bonus – 5 More Tantalizing Recipes on **Glow 15 Unofficial Recipe Book by Karah Westlake!** – *immediately*!

Made in the USA
Middletown, DE
26 June 2018